Strut

Lovingly dedicated to
(beauty + power)^2

my father, John Thomas Tallie
&
my friend, Cheryl Boyce-Taylor

Strut

Mariahadessa Ekere Tallie

Agape Editions
Los Angeles, CA

Published by Agape Editions
http://agapeeditions.com
Los Angeles, CA

Copyright © 2018 by Mariahadessa Ekere Tallie
All rights reserved

Front Cover:
Artwork by Mirlande Jean-Gilles.
Collage is used by kind permission of the artist.
Author's family photograph: photographer unknown.
Image is used by kind permission of the author.

Back Cover:
Author photograph by Dominique Sindayiganza.
Image is used by kind permission of the photographer.

Cover & interior design: Lauren A. Pirosko

Editors: Fox Frazier-Foley & Jasmine An
Associate Editor: Jen Fitzgerald

This book is set in Ahellya Regular and Ahellya Italic.

Agape Editions titles are printed using Lightning Source
and distributed by Ingram Content Group.

This title is also for purchase directly from the publisher.

Library of Congress
Cataloguing-in-Publication Data
Strut // Mariahadessa Ekere Tallie
Library of Congress Control Number 2017949326
Tallie, Mariahadessa Ekere
ISBN 978-1-939675-56-9

10 9 8 7 6 5 4 3 2 1

FIRST EDITION

AGAPE
EDITIONS

Acknowledgments

To the All Good. Ashé.

John and Jewell Tallie, your love is the strongest prayer.
Dominique Sindayiganza, my Nennie, you're a miracle.
Serene, Joy-Shanti, Indigo, "my" finest poems.
Oma, pure steady light.

Jen Fitzgerald, Frank X Walker, Lynn Melnick, sages who helped guide this book here.

Big shout-outs to:

Mellody, John, 8 stars otherwise known as nieces and nephews, my gazillion cousins but especially Jacqui, Jas and Big Man.

Mirlande Jean-Gilles, Sequoia, Azaria, Brett Crenshaw, Iliana Quander, Egypt, Lisa Shears, Leonardo Benzant, Maia, Kyle Richards, Baba Donald Eaton, Muneco, Ina, Andrea, Kyle Smith, Senai, Namdi, Uzo, Malije, Ben, Sarah, Nisrin Omer, Bruce, Amena, Rose Padmore, Sofie, Amali, Carolyn Butts, Maitefa Angaza, Sheila Prevost, Umaimah, Lorenza, Korby, Cheryl Boyce-Taylor, Jaqueline Johnson, Peter Kahn, JP Howard, Ed Toney, EJ Antonio, Shuana Morgan, Enzo Silon Surin, Quincy Troupe, Margaret Troupe, Willie Perdomo, Tyehimba Jess, LaTasha Diggs, Liza Jessie Peterson, Jessica Care Moore. Rest well, Monica Hand. Patricia Milanes, Mark Blickley, Shereen Inayatulla, Mychel Namphy, La Forrest Cope, Rosebud Ben-Oni, Kelli Stevens Kane, Samantha Thornhill, Patricia Spears Jones, Troy Johnson, Ron Kavanaugh, Marcia Wilson, Tony Medina, Ahi Baraka, Kalamu Ya Salaam, Charleen McClure, Len Lawson, Timothy Veit Jones, Angel C Dye, Gabriel Ramirez, Robalu, Gia Shakur, Tracie Morris, Bonafide Rojas, Nadia Alexis, Gary Johnson, Amber Atiya, Marjorie Tesser, Yesenia Montilla, Andrea Walsh, Andy Davis, Fiona, Carol Coonrod, John Coonrod, Rejin Leyes, Georges, Annam Brahma fam, OH Remedies massive, Chataki, Panorama Cafe folks, Guru Health crew.

African Voices, Mosaic, The Watering Hole, Women Writers in Bloom Poetry Salon, The Center for Black Literature, AALBC, Writers Place, Furious Flower, NYFA, Queens Council on the Arts, Center for Book Arts, J Expressions, Queens Book Festival, *IDLEWILD magazine*, World Fellowship Center, IRT Andover.

College and university faculty, staff, and students who have generously hosted me and inspired me.

Fox, Jasmine, Lauren, and Agape Crew.

My gratitude runs deep.

Sincere thanks to the editors of the following publications where many of these poems were first published:

Specter Magazine, The Mom Egg, Badilisha Poetry X-Change, Blind Beggar Press 35th Anniversary Anthology, Women Writers Bloom Poetry Salon Website, Revenge and Forgiveness, The Art of War and Peace, Black Mermaids in Vision and Verse, WSQ: Women's Studies Quarterly, Black Renaissane Noire, North American Review, Minerva Rising, Mosaic, The Pierian, Center for Book Arts Broadside Series, Oya N'Soro, Hysteria, The Missouri Review Soundbooth, Circe's Lament, 90's Meg Ryan, The Breakbeat Poets, Poetry Mail, The Wide Shore, Newtown Literary, No, Dear.

Table of Contents

Madness	1
Global Warming Blues	2
New York Talk	3
Mama Haiku 1	5
Learning To Swim	6
Mama Haiku 2	8
Blue Libation	9
Unhyphenated Souls	10
Mami Wata	11
Polaris	12
The Bembe	13
Who Decides?	15
Garment Working Women	17
Memory	18
I Want to Take Him	19
Blaze	20
What I Remember	21
Lady	24
First of All, It's Hard to Write About You Using Lined Paper, But I'll Try	25
The Day I Knew I Loved You	27
Pencil	29
After the Ansel Adams Exhibit	30
My Love for Him Ends the Occupation	31
Give and Take	33
Brazen Hussy Blues	34

Rain	35
Breakin' Up Blues	36
Note From A Loving Wife	37
Real Woman's Survival Haiku	38
Who Knows Very Well Who He Is	39
Why You've Loved Me Ever Since You Started Thinking in English	40
Sunday	41
Gap-Toothed Woman	42
Paper Bag Poems	44
Inspiration	45
We Still Don't Know	46
3 Snapshots	47
Sovereign	48
The Clean Earth Conference Blues Haiku	49
Infinity	50
Final Quartet	51
Homage to my Breasts	52
Ancient	53
Migration Blues	54
Old Man Haiku	55
Strut	56
Daughter Haiku	57
Freed Verses	58
Possible	59
Ars Poetica	62
Notes	65

Our crown has already been bought and paid for.
All we have to do is wear it.
—James Baldwin

Madness

runs in my family.
Dish hurling, knife wielding,
hard drinking, blind loving.

Nothing flows through our veins
blood stomps, tramples,
stampedes, could crack stone.

Ask how I make decisions

it depends on the wind's shimmy
whether I dream 6 or 9
patterns of coffee grinds

my foundation cracked
with the whip's first snap
I'm just trying to get my name back.

It's why my hips move the way they do,
why I'm second-line New Orleans boisterous,
why I listen to the dark,

I break
commit myself
to the white room
of the page,

I write my own
damn prescriptions.

Global Warming Blues

The ocean had a laugh
when it saw the shore
I said the ocean had a big big laugh
when it saw the shore
it pranced on up the boardwalk
and pummeled my front door

There's no talking to the water
full of strength and salt
no, there's no bargaining with water
so full of strength and salt
I'm a Mama working two jobs
global warming ain't my fault

I said *Please water, I recycle*
got a garden full of greens
I said *looka here I compost*
got a garden full of greens
water say *big men drill and oil spill*
we both know what that means

Now my town is just a river
bodies floatin, water's high
my town is just a river
but I'm too damn mad to cry
seem like for Big Men's livin
little folks have got to die

   seems like for Big Men's livin
   little folks have got to die

New York Talk

Didn't I tell you
about stairs wearing
fresh coats
of piss,
about gunshot
lullabies,
about my best friend
miscarrying
on her mother's couch
at 16,
men like boobytraps
waiting to blow us up,
my kin floating
down the block
on a cloud of crack,
endless rivers of wine
flowing through my home.

I needed swords
& broken glass & soldiers
an army of words charging from me

speech of survival

speech of renting the land
stolen from your grandfather
& cleaning offices built
on your grandma's grave

mouths like middle passage
& migration, peach trees
& projects

understand
why I craved the weight
of curses on my tongue?

Shooting syllables,
mothafucka-wrapped dreams
like armor.

Mama Haiku 1

Packed to leave this country
called life—my mother
was stopped at the border

Learning To Swim

She was the baby of the family,
curious and neon
magic unraveling her singing braids.
There was music coming off of her
violins, batas, pianos, and castanetas,
sounds that reminded momma of sin.

Sienna sunflower girl
knee high
southern tinged
tangos and rumbas tickling her feet,
imagine
the first time the branch of the peach tree
ripped her skin,
she'd been caught
moving to some rhythm
moving to some rhythm
not born of the church.

Her sound, her scent,
her earthspeak
brought the hands,
the belts, the switches

down
she tried,
when she left their house,
she tried to conjure her dance again
hear the whispers under her feet

she pulled watercolors around her waist
wore amber and amethyst on wrists and shoulders
chanted and wound her way through jazz,
but no one could read the smoke signals
of her cigarettes

Death would be sweeter than any of this.

When we met
she was 35
and I was newly born
she was still drowning
but she gave me studios to dance in
trumpets
screaming magentas
muted blues
congas
tarot cards
modeling clay
She kept judgment in a locked box
too high for me to reach.

She stepped aside
my mother stepped aside
She'd evacuated her own dreams
courted death many times.

When I met her
she was still drowning
but somehow she took me
to the water
and somehow
She taught me to swim.

Mama Haiku 2

She sighs cigarette
clouds   nicotine halos float
eyes   embers flicker

Blue Libation
(For Walter Wright Sr. and Mariah Wright)

I lit the candle of poem
in Mississippi & in the silence
of a blue morning, libation
rolled down my cheeks.

It was the cotton sheets.
My great-great grandparents'

hands & lives
bent over small, tough
clouds. I slept
in the softness of my hotel
room, wrapped in a whisper
of my history.

Unhyphenated Souls

No accident
some say our sanity
is chained to ocean floor.
Those ships. Those ships.
The water
saw all that was us
taken whole
taken circular
taken out of concert with sun.

That was us.
Thighs pried.
Tongues chopped.
Water eulogizing.

Should have shifted the tide,
should have made the journey impossible

a wall of water rising, keeping ships on shore.

Should have drowned them who believed
there was a *them*

Let us keep our unpatoised mouths
unhyphenated souls.

Mami Wata

    Some chose
    ocean floor.

    Wrapped their breaths
    in a siren song,

    opened their lungs
    to spirit frayed
    freedom

    Mami Wata
    knows their names.

Polaris

Followed our higherselves
to freedom

        Great grandma twinkling
                    that way
            across the night

Under midnight's quilt of coal
hushed feet
stitched vision:
laughing daughters
    spines haughty as baobabs

        Rifled woman
        vast mirror of oracle sky:
        dark
        cool
        burning
        free

Shedding greed's gravity
conspired with winking suns
to wear again our secret names

Why we look up

Believe.

The Bembe

Chorus of city dwellers
fanning ourselves in a basement
boasting tropical heat,

water of shekere.

Randy
   pours
    the
     rum
    of
    his
   voice
  into
Ogun's
  thirsty
   ear,

tree and animal speak again
when Baba's hands translate scripture
to rhythm,

agogo unravels a thin veil
between us & the unseen.

        This basement dizzy
        with praise   giddy with
          Movement,   echoes

            across land & water

                a far flung living room,
              courtyard greetings exchanged

                in Patois   Portuguese
                abichuelas y arroz heaped
                on paper plates, dark hands wrapping

brown spirits around tired shoulders   doing away
with slavery,

                    where family was broken
                        dragged away to begin the journey

        this exact moment happens.

            A remembering
    solid and present as smooth river stones
            in rebellious bellies.

Who Decides?

Afternoon
filled with chill and silver
I put my girls to bed

the woman on the radio spoke
with a voice like cracking porcelain

murder
killed
killing
dead

I looked at my daughters
on the verge of sleep,
heard the woman on the radio
sole survivor
in her family
Rwandan genocide
mother
father
six siblings

killed

she ran with her grandmother
from machetes
corpses in her dreams

killed
murdered
dead

my children sleeping
amidst talk of Tutsis
like their grandfather
being cut down

amidst talk of Belgium
the land of their grandmother

my children's blood
running warm through their bodies, the blood
of the talking woman's
mother spilling in the street

who decides?

Garment Working Women

Bengali woman
haloed in smoke we refuse
to wear your death in style

Consumer activism?
an oxymoron
windowless workers

Bengali women's
ashes in pockets of jeans
factory graveyard

Memory

    1.

Your eyes are full
of stories, I lean
in closer to hear.

    2.

You brush your memories
across my lips. Everything
tastes like tears.

I Want to Take Him

from the closed
door of his mama.

Her eyes on the other eight,
or the TV,
or her man,
while the boy breaks.

It is his arm again.
The second time
in six months
in the same place.

He is eight
and his voice is pure water
and his eyes drink love.

His heart is not yet like his arm
his heart is not yet like the door of his mama.

Blaze

You sat
in the blandness of my winter
& set fire to the snow

What I Remember

(I. The First Phone Conversation)

Our words were ripe, wild
raspberries chosen
carefully on a green afternoon.

> I wanted you
> to change the soundtrack
> of my heart. Unbirth Billie's
> moan from my throat, help
> me speak honey
> again.

Your words
were palms pressed
in prayer, a hand
open & offered to me.

(II. The First Date: You Bought a Mango)

You carried the sun
gently, sweet Haitian
rain in your palm.

dawn's sugary flesh
against the midnight
of your hand.

I remember the mirror
of uprooted
fruit.

I remember
the tears you spoke,
orange candles in your basement,
how I listened to your footsteps.

Our hands were quiet
      then,
we memorized each other
like scripture.

(III. Nothing Left but the Fall)

      Days running our
      fingers over each others'
      words.

plates of yasa and Joloff rice
afternoons
      reciting Shange
      & Perdomo,

coaxing the light back.
      breathing into me
red candles flickering
roses, morning glories.

Did I ever thank you?
Not for the gifts of food
      or books

but for the gift of you?

(IV. Fin)

How to say good-bye to water,
to ocean, to salt, to us, something pure
breaking,
  waves of you
still hummed in my skin.

Lady

Lady, what is beneath your skin
seemingly satisfied with one
uncomplicated man?
You've signed his name
onto yours/woven two lives
into a fine garment.

Tell me
does he unzip your howl
trace the etymology of your tears
is he fluent in your black lace laughter

does anywhere you go together
become rich with the fragrance of lovers
does your hand brushing his
make all the dust
settle?

Lady, I am red clay
swirling   I am a trembling match
licking a scripture's certainty.
I walk alone and unravel holy things.
I can chew a good man to the gristle
I scare myself everyday
a hunter dances beneath my skin.

Lady, have you ever seen a tornado
in your mirror?
How did you cage her
before she smashed
everything?

First of All, It's Hard to Write About You Using Lined Paper, But I'll Try

it's in the margins
isn't it?

>   some black invisible
>   way out place where
>   water flows up
>   & lilies bloom
>   in clouds
>   is where we touch

not here
on this planet called perpetually
out of her name   this rumor
jungle   this porcelain
nepotistic maze. how could
this space hold our beauty?
free the unshackled alphabet
of what we'd be?

>   i've got to have you
>   where the sea
>   is the color of dragon fruit
>   fertile soil is indigo
>   & everywhere
>   whispers & thighs
>   are all day

>   i've got to have you
>   between puffs of lavender
>   & artemisia-inspired dreams
>   Audre Lorde onstage with
>   Sun Ra & Minnie Ripperton

      where manna falls
      from our kiss &
      community is fed
      & sun never leaves
      a Black boy's eyes

      (you play in the mirror of my hair
      see a hero in the reflection)

don't visit me here
this valley of shame

          build us a   mansion of touch
          a rebellious stanza that doesn't
          know its place   marches
          out of books   rides its own
          sound
                  eternal.

The Day I Knew I Loved You

1.

convinced myself to forget
your name became secret music
tucked between my hips

2.

what love lets a man hover?
here is the dark door
here is the sweet aroma
here is rice
here is children's laughter
come, eavesdrop on this life

3.

forgot myself
your music name
secret

4.

prayed: if we choose
this collision
let him unlock his chest
treasure of rubies & afro picks
let him remember sugar & freeze tag
erase his Daddy's fire hands

let us be a wild undiscovered spring
let us sip each other's magic

5.

No
let us gulp
drown
resurface
reborn
& strong enough
to walk away

Pencil

There are small braveries that do not feel brave.
I'm going to start to write in pencil now,
because nothing is etched in stone/permanent
because my heart is stronger than my wrists
& I must.

Moment of bravery?
Deciding to do it/to write
        I've said this before
Another?
Kissing a mouth on a corner on a public street
in the sun.

We're going to have a problem, he said.

Heat bearing down/giving birth to a relationship
that would wring us both out
lay us out to bleach us/bleach not
our blackness/our browness/which is oceanic
& will cover earth one day
not bleach that unstoppable
beauty/but bleach out the ink we defined ourselves in
when we signed our names in books & on paper
under definitions of who we thought we were,

we are not that.
I am no longer ink.

I can erase any version of me.

After the Ansel Adams Exhibit

1.

juniper bark   dark
skin of an ancient story
asking my name again

2.

sequoia roots,   soft
scripture   Mama's hands when she
finally sleeps

3.

waterfalls remind
him   my bare shoulders
aroma of mischief

4.

tasting unwritten
poems   salt
between thighs

5.

silken sea's rumba
my breathing
when I come

My Love for Him Ends the Occupation

My love for him:

inevitable as death
insistent mosquito
redwood roots

a memory in the blood   his glance & honeyed dew
saunters down my thighs   yes   there is a graceless orange howl
that escapes my throat   pulls night curtains
across the sky   behind it the stage is bare
unset unsettled   yes
Black people know how to do more than die
our kisses steeped long & patient
we conjured each other up   unsettling that we   love like this
move invaders out with raw silk feeling   agogo tongues
uncolonize ourselves with genuine north star touch

I get my land back
now & then when we move in sync
40 acres of velvet soil   beds of collard greens
rows of ecstatic tomatoes   dignified yellow corn
(I'm not the mule)
out of my house   hopeless feeling like the weather
in Leeds   out of my house.
The occupation is over
our loving moves back in.

Give and Take

1.

You live in my bones.
Even I cannot evict
you. Slowly, you pack.

2.

Pull your concertos off
the hangers, fold your women
& your prophecy, take your
half-truths off the lower shelves,
put your laughter back in its
garment bag, collect your wisdom
from the high hall shelves, take
your ego from the hamper, gather
your voice from the living room, your
sweat from the linen.

3.

I will drink something vintage
when you leave.
I will paint the walls
deep orange.
I will fill the rooms with frankincense,
Sanskrit, and Be-bop.

4.

The mirror shows me
the one thing you left.

The soundlessness in my chest
reminds me of the last
thing you took.

Brazen Hussy Blues

I like a man who's handy
makes my house feel good as new
he don't need no tool kit
when we hammer, nail, and screw

some gals are fine with one man
I've always needed two
cause what the first can't handle
the second sho can do

once I get my two men
I go find number three
morning, noon, and night
I got some sweet thing next to me

people say I'm brazen
I say *well that ain't news*
you at home washing dishes
wishin you was in my shoes

cryin over some man?
none can have my heart to bruise,
there ain't no such thing
as the brazen hussy blues

Rain

gliding timbales
tap routine of clouds
guaguanco dew

where are you?
where are you?

meant to pry me
from loneliness
that bright & ancient
star

Where are your midnight cravings
your three a.m. fingers
your tongue erasing the shore

where are your
gentle rosewood shoulders
our journeying to planets
undiscovered until the curve
of your back
urgent road rising
between your thighs.

Water giggling on my roof
surrenders to the earth's mouth.
I'm as solitary as any woman
as solitary as any woman
even with you.

Breakin' Up Blues

Been loving you so long,
forgot that love's a thrill
I've consumed you, Baby
& now I had my fill.

Note From A Loving Wife

The dishes all want to break,
my love
one by one
they wriggle from my hands
shattering in unsorry pieces

leave him cries
the cracked bowl
you are too much whispers
a shard of plate
too good jagged mouth
of glass *to be here*

your very own dishes,
betrayed you, my love.
spoons beat your secrets
'til they bent in fatigue

so when you come home
with her scent in your hair
and you walk from room
to room finding no sign
of me, keep your shoes on

particularly in the kitchen.
My freedom might get
stuck in your feet.

Real Woman's Survival Haiku

Every woman's
got to know how to strum her
way to afterglow.

Who Knows Very Well Who He Is

It took four hours for me
to stop tingling where you touched,
for orchids to quiet whispering
between my thighs

you rose, a morning prayer
a bouquet of salt and honey,
swept through me like a tide of bata

where do you come from, magic man?
you remind me I am sacred
ask and offer, replace
what was taken

where do you come from, magic man?
your breath makes
each morning holy.

Why You've Loved Me Ever Since You Started Thinking in English
(For Dominique)

There are no soft
sounds, no words
like pillows, plump
vowels ripe sweet
juicy sliding down
your chin, your neck
there, there where my lips
meet the hollow below
the apple. My English
gives you what your
language does not

cotton, Coltrane, candied
yams, marches, sit-ins,
panthers, black, Black
Black Love and space,
spirits draped in honey,
oh oh oh my God gospel
in bed (and Sunday mornings)
orchids, Sun-Ra, collard greens,
swagger, collage of tragedy
and dignity, Romare, romance and salt
water, house parties, hands
on hips, *don't let them get your
fingernails or your hair,* trumpets,
raucous, masks, tears, laughter,
volume, bass

loving me
hums you
closer to unburying
the root.

Sunday

All week
my hands are small
brown cyclones

sudsy water, braids, grocery bags,
cast-iron skillets, collard greens,
shirts and folding, broom,
mop, dust pan, chalkboard, shoelaces,
sweet potatoes, cups, sheets, bowls.

all week
my hands are brown birds
guiding a tiny flock

come Sunday
the hands need rest,
need holding.

Now I understand
why my foremothers
embraced Sunday
like I would a lover:

eager, radiant,
ready to be filled.

Gap-Toothed Woman
(Golden shovel poem)

Wear the brave stockings of night black lace
and strut down the streets with paint on my face.
—Gwendolyn Brooks

They brace themselves. I wear
my gap-toothed smile, the
mouth of beauty. Journeys of brave
women, salty & blue. Fulani hands mending stockings,
nursing strangers, stitching lives. Bleeding women of
cane & cotton, forced women dreading night,
blues women, salty & bleeding, surviving & black.

These teeth? An inheritance more inviting than lace
the driver says &
he knows I am his stolen sister, strut
of my eyes, spaced stars in the sky of my mouth travel back & down
strands of tangled heritage, the
me before these shores, these streets.

They brace themselves, teeth & words aligned with what shipped them here. They paint smiles & deference on their lips. My gap-toothed rebellion is an altar. My ancestors gather in the hills of my face.

Paper Bag Poems

"These poets use being black to write about larger subjects."
—Charles Rowell

Fulla field hollers,
rifles, unrefined
liquor,

my poems can't pass
paper bag tests.

Blueprints for surviving
architecture of grief.

There is nothing larger
than the night sky
of our blood.

Broken bones of teardrops,
three generations of raw
throated women.

Fists rising from these pages.

Inspiration

Midnight slips off her robe of stars,
places ripe slices of moon
between my lips. Song finds me.

We Still Don't Know
(for Jimi Hendrix)

Who was that hoodoo
wrapped in turquoise
and scripture?

That priest of earthquakes
conjuring white buffalos
through amplified oracle wails.

fire

Tuned ears heard flames
the volcano rained down,
batons and dogs
rained down,
fire hoses and bullets
rained down.

freedom

The shaman was indigo
was bluesman
was raven
was watching
watching
composing mantras
of aloe and steel.

Who was that whisperer wrapped
in rainbows and sand?

Genius.
Genie.
Jimi.

3 Snapshots
(for Marvin Gaye)

1.

Sing belt stings, loose
noose of daddy's name, high off
pusherman manna

2.

Broken beat Whole note
tongue deep in pulpit of thigh
Holy roller testify

3.

How could we make love
to your slow dance
with suicide?

Sovereign
(For Gil-Scott Heron)

Fraying silk of voice
a flag flying over broken
hoping territory of us.

Why couldn't he
greet tomorrow? Rest
in the home of our eyes?

What pain settled,
occupied the land
of his vast heart?

Who colonized
his joy?

How did he
battle to keep
his tongue?

The Clean Earth Conference Blues Haiku

Experts fly in from
everywhere, polluting
land and sea and air

Infinity
(for Amiri Baraka)

fog swept through my marrow
bones sagged
where did he go?

silver air got sliced
sky fell   revealed
its glistening innards

we inched our way
through Newark morning
laced with memory & salt.

Balm of our togetherness
bomb of his stillness
This is a stick-up.
Amiri, get out of the coffin.

passed around a flask
of loss   everyone sipped.

There is no end

Final Quartet
(for Yasmeen)

1.

Wearing the name
of fragrant flowers
you gave your voice to the sea.

2.

Depression   three sharp
syllables grinding
women's bones.

3.

In frozen water
you unpacked your trembling
where were we?

4.

Are you in the seagull's
cry? Is that your voice
rolling down my cheeks?

Homage to my Breasts
(after Lucille Clifton)

these breasts are no longer stargazers
even alert   they can't look a man
in the eye. they sighed milk
for two girl children who grew round
& learned the alphabet on pearls of mama dew,
these breasts became bread, then lowered
their dough heads, watched the children
crawl & walk. these breasts erased
memory of tongues craving
different food, two bowls of fire
cupped in a hungry man's hands.

Ancient
(for Tish Benson)

Rainbow draped in brown,
arched across time,

field hollers, ocean &
broken shackles collide
in your voice,

ancient seed, sprouting
the language of hurricanes,

carrying medicine pouches called
poems. Buffalos charge
across your tongue.

Migration Blues

    I left my Daddy
    the okra and the trees

    earned myself a few degrees.

    I'd give back those letters
    put down my pen
    if I could just hear
    Daddy's voice again.

Old Man Haiku

Old man slowly
walking to the other side
his daughters gather

Strut

After birthing twins
my friend whittled
herself back to hourglass.
She describes the black sand,
her turquoise bikini, pride,
seeing herself strut again.

I will never wear one again
I say. Then show.
The pot, the loose skin,
the lightning bolts, the rain
streaks across my belly.

I wear the turbulent body
of a stranger. Sharp,
soft until the hill
of broken muscle
announcing life
beyond my life.

I thank my bones,
my broken muscles.
I thank the woman I was,
and the woman I am.

Slowly, I learn
to strut again.

Daughter Haiku

Papery pink blossoms
tickle the starched grey sky
my daughter giggles

Freed Verses

Old folks speak to me
through mouth of wind,
throat of cowries,

tell me they saw my coming.
My strange preoccupation
with putting things on paper,
my companionship with night.

They plotted generations,
spoke every name,
etched themselves in my palms.

Old folks speak to me
through bones that rattle
like bottled thunder,

tell me
before pen or paper
they secured my birth
with poems written
on edges of raised
machetes.

Possible
(for Amiri Baraka)

out of the box   they spring
out of the narrowness of yesterday & some bleak
projected tomorrow

impossible men

outlawed drum of their hearts
punishable dance of their breath
our loving them is the forbidden religion

impossible   Black & looking the world straight in its eyes
not smiling/making mouths cushions
for someone's fear to rest on/not smiling

moving through streets   hills   universities   forests
like they gotta right

alchemy of voice   ideas & soul   taking up deserved space
creating it.

Impossible   seducing language out of its corset
into shimmy & groin

***

blood jail burying the young
something darker than blue moaned
through his life's veins
still, he ain't forget the graceful sea
of jitterbug   sweet rivers
of Smokey   how to reawaken
laughter in our eyes

insurrection of his tenderness
surrender to the work
of love   not just the romance

***

he's impossible
exasperated arms flung
shaking heads   closed doors
establishment wallets shut

but he is
& is possible
& is widening possibility
right here.

Ars Poetica

May the poems be
      the lifting of heavy things
      the putting down of burden
      the excavation of laughter & true names
      the fists
      the inhale
      the wild water
      the knife
      the beginning

Notes

"Mami Wata"
Mami Wata is a West African Spirit of the ocean.

"The Bembe"
A bembe is a celebration of forces of nature, called Orishas, that originated in Nigeria, Benin, and Togo. There is drumming, singing, and dancing aimed at calling the Forces down to earth to speak to those gathered.

Ogun is the Orisha of cities, iron, technology, and war.

"Why You've Loved Me Ever Since You Started Dreaming In English"
Romare refers to Romare Bearden, celebrated collage artist and painter.

"Gap-Toothed Woman"
Golden shovel is a poetic form created by Terrance Hayes. The poet takes a line from a poem and uses each word to end her/his lines. I used a line from Gwendolyn Brooks' "A Song in the Front Yard."

"Infinity"
Italicized words from Saul Williams' remarks at Amiri Baraka's funeral.

"Ancient"
Tish Benson is Leticia Benson, radiant author of *Wild Like That Strong Stuff Smelling Good*.

www.ingramcontent.com/pod-product-compliance
Lightning Source LLC
Chambersburg PA
CBHW050206130526
44591CB00035B/2336